A Gent for the *Soul*

Providing comfort and reassurance in times of need

Daniela
Sending love & hugs
Lindsay x

Lindsay Coldrick

ISBN: 978-1-9162805-0-2

Contents

Foreword

31/05/2018

I want to influence and show others the way to live a life that is honest and true. To support them in their daily lives. To give them the tools to take responsibility for their emotional wellbeing. To encourage them to be the best that they can be. To bring awareness, not only to them but to their families and their children. To cater for their emotional needs. To reassure when times are hard. To enlighten. To share the message. To share love. To share light. For everyone to enjoy a gentle hug for the soul. To move together towards a world of peace and enlightenment. To bring together the worlds of business and spirituality. To be aware. To be conscious. To feel. To feel alive. To feel a part of this world. To unite. A community. A tribe. Peace and Calm. For decisions to be made from love and light. To not fear. To be decisive and trust their intuition. To feel calm. To feel content. To work together, to come together. Together we stand, as the souls and light we are. In our place. We stand. We live. We love.

This book is dedicated to my friend, Lisa.

Acknowledgements

I WOULD LIKE TO thank my mam and dad firstly for supporting me and being there always. My sister Joanne, for keeping me grounded. My 92-year-old grandma, who always listens to me chatting about spirits and the Universe. My son and daughter who are my why.

I am so grateful to Chris and Lisa who have been there for me, inspiring and coaching over the last year. To my tribe, Siv, Cathy, Mel, Mariola, Virginia and Daniella who have been true friends. To Felix for introducing me to Reiki back in 2002. To Rachael for teaching me Access Bars.

Thank you to Gayle Johnson who helped me to put my story in order and refined it. Elaine White, who has been a mentor without knowing it. Louise Mason for guiding me on the marketing path. To Rosalind Beardshaw for my beautiful image on the cover. To the Lonestar for the cover design.

Thank you to all those who read my book, fed back and became part of my launch team.

Thank you to all those who have been put in my path for me to learn and grow from.

Thank you to the Universe for providing me with everything I need.

Thank you.

Introduction

Building your Spiritual Toolbox

I HAVE A SPIRITUAL toolbox that I dip in and out of depending on what life throws at me. In this box are tools to help me ease conflict, to be brave enough to make decisions, to move forward when I'm at a fork in the road, to support me in life and to enable me to ask for support from others.

I wrote this book to share these tools with you. I can honestly say that my life is easier, more fulfilling and more exciting now I'm making the most of these tools. They took me years to learn, and I want you to have access to that sense of purpose, fulfilment and excitement now.

A little of my spiritual journey

Finding and getting comfortable with these tools has been a long process for me. I first learned about Reiki in 2002 in Hong Kong when my friend Felix came back buzzing after a weekend retreat. He asked if he could put his hands on my back and I remember feeling this intense heat.

It took me six years to take things further. I was working in a stressful job with a major retailer and had just gone through a fairly intense breakup with a boyfriend. I needed something to help me with my emotions. I remembered Reiki. The first Reiki treatment I had I didn't feel anything. A waste of money I thought.

However, I kept a journal and I realised that actually it had done something. I felt calmer, more relaxed and more energised. When the Reiki teacher asked me if I wanted to learn Reiki Level 1 I jumped at the chance. It gave me new tools to help balance my emotions at work. I found it easier to make decisions and started using my intuition.

In 2008 I also went to see a medium. I had never been to see a medium before so wasn't sure what to expect. I was invited to her home. She switched on the recorder and started talking. She described my grandad, who had passed seven years previously and my granddad's neighbour, Ethel. She not only described them but also brought through memories they had of my dad and me. She told me I was going to meet someone and have a whirlwind romance. She said I would meet them, move in, get engaged, get married, have kids. It would happen very quickly. At the time I was happily single so had no idea what she was talking about. Towards the end she asked why she was seeing Angel Cards with me. I said I had no idea. I honestly had no idea at the time what they were!

When I got home I went on Google and bought myself a pack of Doreen Virtue Angel Cards. I started using the angel cards for guidance and reassurance. I started doing a daily card to see what I needed to know that day. Nine times out of ten it was right. If it wasn't I would get the same card the next day.

I met my husband at my Reiki Level 1 course. We fell in love, got engaged, got married, got pregnant twice and set up our own business.

Navigating new motherhood, our relationship and setting up a business was stressful. The tools I had learned helped me through all of these big milestones in my life.

On October 24th 2016 (my birthday) one of my best friends, Lisa, died of cancer. I can't describe the grief I felt for her. It was so raw. I realised how numb I had become to my emotions and I didn't want that anymore. I felt detached from life and like I was flat-lining. I knew I couldn't carry on doing that.

Shortly afterwards, my ex and I decided to separate. Coping with bereavement then the emotional and practical turmoil of splitting up whilst looking after my children tested me to the limit. I had to use all of the tools in my spiritual toolbox to get me through.

And that's when I finally, truly saw how life-changing these tools are. When we face crisis, life is hard. But we do have choices. And by choosing to let these tools help me I'm building my life consciously, with guidance, with support. It's not always easy but I can honestly say I feel happy, fulfilled and on purpose in ways I haven't before. And that's what I want for you, too.

Who is this book for?

If you are going through a crisis, be it bereavement or divorce, or if it's simply that you're in a rut and your everyday life is not what you'd hoped it would be, I would love to work with you and share these tools. Once you've learnt them, they are yours for life. And I don't want it to take you over 15 years, like it did me. I have included in the book not only what the tools are but how you can use them too. I have also included the hashtag #AGentlehugforthesoul as I want people to come together and share their stories, to share how you have used the tools in your life, to feedback and to create a community. So, whether you are on Twitter or Instagram you can use this hashtag to share.

You will notice that there are a few paragraphs in the book written in italic. Prior to writing these pieces I meditated and asked spirit to come through and help me write something for this book. These words aren't mine, but the words from one of my spirit guides, whose name is Budmit.

This book will give you some tools which are free and readily available now. You can start building your own spiritual toolbox today! Feel free to start reading the chapter you're most drawn to. This is a resource for you to use as you need: let your interest and intuition guide you. However, if you're not sure where to start, let's talk energy first!

Chapter 1: Understanding and Using Energy

In this chapter we look at what energy is and how understanding that you are an energetic being can help you in life. We look at how we are built emotionally and how others' energy can affect us.

Auras

You are not just a physical being. You are an energy being. Surrounding our physical body, we have another body of energy known as the auric field, or aura. Each person's aura has its own distinctive energy signature. Its energetic vibrational frequencies are unique. Our aura contains energy centres known as chakras, which I will talk about later. There are seven layers contained in our auras.

Why is it important that I learn about my aura?

In order to understand yourself as an energy being, learning about the different layers of the aura can significantly help you. Everything that has happened so far in your life is collected in your aura. Your stories and your experiences are there. Having a clear and vibrant aura helps you to attract what you want in your life. Having an aura which is heavy and full of 'stuff' that you haven't dealt with, can make it more difficult to attract what you want in your life. So, what are the different layers?

Etheric Body: This is closest to our physical bodies. It is where we hold everything we touch. It can often look milky white.

Emotional Body: Where we store how we feel about things emotionally, especially in relation to our self.

Mental Body: How agile we are in our minds and how rationally we think.

Higher Mental Body: How you love yourself and others around you. It is about relationships at all levels and how you deal with them.

Spiritual Body: To do with knowing where you fit into the universe as a whole.

Causal Body: How you love unconditionally; not only those you are close to, but also in a larger, universal context.

Ketheric Body: This links us to the Divine and our higher self.

Some people can see auras and sometimes it is possible to feel someone's aura. If you immediately feel comfortable with someone it's because their auras are similar to yours. If you feel instantly repelled it is because the vibration of your aura conflicts with theirs.

I first saw an aura when I was about 19 or 20. I was sat in a friend's living room and we were talking to her grandma. As I was looking at her grandma there was this green colour around her. I thought my eyes were playing tricks on me. I looked around the room and couldn't find anything green. You know sometimes when you stare at something long enough then look away that colour is still there? There wasn't anything green so I looked at her again and the green was still there. When she left the room, I turned to my friend and said I think I've just seen your grandma's aura. She looked at me then cracked up laughing. I didn't know what it was as I'd never seen one before.

When I was 28 I had my next experience of seeing an aura. I went to an Introduction to Crystals workshop. As I was looking at the teacher I could see this green energy above her head again.

Certain colours can dominate a person's aura, which can tell an aura reader (someone who can see auras easily and reads them) a lot about that person's character. The analysis of the aura is combined with the reader's own intuition to tell you a bit more about yourself.

What do the colours mean?

Red: Desire, vitality, power, the urge to win, to have success, intensity of experience, action, doing, love of sports, struggle, competition, force of will, leadership, strength, courage, passion, eroticism, earthiness, practicality, desire for possessions, sense of adventure, the survival instinct.

Orange: Creativity, the emotions, confidence, ability to relate to others in an open and friendly manner, sociability, intuition or gut feeling. The ability to reach out and extend one's self towards others.

Yellow: Sunny and enthusiastic, cheerful, bright, great sense of humour and fun, optimism, intellectuality, openness to new ideas, happiness, warmth, relaxation. Uninhibited expansiveness, release of burdens, problems and restrictions. Talent for organization. Hope and expectation, inspiration. People with yellow auras encourage and support others by naturally being themselves; they radiate like the sun and they also may have a great ability to analyse complex concepts.

Green: Perseverance, tenacity, firmness, patience, sense of responsibility and service, self- assertiveness, high ideals and aspirations, dedication, puts high value on work and career. Ambitious desire for respectability and personal attainment, deeply focused and adaptable.

Blue: Depth of feeling, devotion, loyalty, trust, desire to communicate. Puts great importance on personal relationships.

Empathetic. May be a dreamer or have artistic ability. Possibly tend to put the needs of others before their own and may have the ability to meditate, and live in the moment. Blue may be emotionally sensitive, intuitive, inwardly focused, may enjoy solitude, non-competitive activities, be receptive and desire unity, peace, love and affection in relationships with others. They need a calm and tranquil environment.

Violet or Purple: Magical, original, tends to be unconventional, often has psychic abilities, unusual charisma and charm, the uncommon ability to make their dreams come true, or manifest their desires in the material world, wish to charm and delight others and can easily connect with higher planes of consciousness. Playful, non-judgemental, tolerant of others' eccentricities. Sensitive and compassionate. "Purples" appreciate tenderness and kindness in others. Not especially practical, they tend to prefer to live in a dream world of their own creation. Dark violet could indicate a need to take charge of their life, or perhaps, that the person needs time to spiritually ground him/herself.

Turquoise or White: Spiritually motivated, the ability to be open and receptive to the divine, or spiritual world. Can merge with All That Is. Probably unconcerned with worldly matters or ambition. Inner illumination, cosmic wisdom characterises the white energy. Young children, energy workers, and intense meditators often will show bright white in their auras.

You may find you see a blend of colours, or just a speck or a flash of green or purple. Factors that influence the colour of an aura are physical condition, emotions, level of consciousness, thoughts, and physical surroundings. Your aura doesn't stay the same over your lifetime, as you learn and grow your aura changes. Through meditation and raising your vibration your aura colours will start to change.

Be aware of yourself as an energetic being rather than a physical being. We aren't JUST made up of our physical body.

In the movie 'Dirty Dancing' Johnny tells Baby, "This is my space and this is yours". Sometimes people can invade our space and it makes us feel uncomfortable. Or the opposite can happen: you might meet someone and feel instantly at ease with them. Your energy vibrations will be on a similar level. I was in a bank recently waiting in a queue, this chap arrived behind me and just got a little bit too close. I could feel that his energy wasn't good so took two steps away from him. He didn't notice but the cashier did. I explained to him when I got to the counter that his energy hadn't resonated with mine and I didn't feel comfortable around him. He smiled and nodded as if to say I see. I don't know if he did.

PRACTICAL TIP

How to see auras

Everyone can see an aura; it's not a gift for specific people. The easiest way to do it is to get someone to stand against a plain white/cream background. Stand about three metres (ten feet) away. Look above the person's head. Just above. They can close their eyes if they don't feel comfortable with you staring at them for a period of time. Allow your eyes to relax. You may begin to see a faint white line around the person's body. What can sometimes happen is that as soon as you see something your brain can shut it down. You get excited that you have 'seen' energy. Breathe, relax and try again.

If you don't have a friend who feels comfortable with you staring at them try using a plant to begin with. Plants are made up of energy too and have a similar life force energy surrounding them.

Feel the aura. Another exercise you can do is to hold your two hands together and pull them apart ever so slightly. You may start to feel a pull between your hands. Experiment with moving your hands apart and together again. Or ask a friend to lie down and place your hands as close to that person's body as possible without touching them. Work your way along the body to see if you can feel a change in any particular area. Move your hands up into the air. You might feel a heaviness or tingling. Practise and let me know how you get on.

Protecting our energies

When we start working on ourselves and raising our own vibration through meditation or self-work the last thing we want is for someone to come crashing in and pull us down. This is where grounding and protecting our energies come in.

I was working in a large supermarket as a manager when I first learnt about grounding and protecting my energy. I was stressed and not managing my stress very well. I wasn't always nice to my staff, and that wasn't the real me. I learned how to ground and protect my energies in my Reiki Level 1 course and this is a great tool for everybody to learn.

You know sometimes when you wake up after a great night's sleep, you feel really positive and happy? But you might have a husband/wife/partner who has had a really crappy night sleep. The first thing they do is grunt at you when you wish them a cheery morning, your energy gets sapped a little bit. You wake up and head downstairs and make the kids' breakfast. You make them coco pops and they come downstairs saying they wanted toast instead, another piece of your positive energy is sapped. You do the school run and get to work. The first person to come and chat to you complains that they are having a dreadful day, they hate the new boss and wish they were at home. That final piece of positive energy that you woke up with has gone.

You start to feel tired and drained, you start snapping at people and go home feeling knackered. Why? Because everyone has taken a piece of your energy from you. This is where grounding and protecting your energy comes in. How do you do this? Read on...

PRACTICAL TIP

How to ground yourself and protect your energy

First thing in the morning when you get up sit on the edge of the bed with your feet flat on the floor. Close your eyes. Imagine tree roots coming out of your feet. Imagine them going down to the centre of the earth. As they go down they grow bigger and stronger. Eventually they hit the centre of the earth which is a beautiful orange. Now imagine that your tree roots are soaking up the orange colour and the orange is travelling back up through your roots. It is going higher and higher until the orange colour enters your feet and goes up your calves, your thighs, through your hips and stomach, through your chest and neck, up through your head and out the top of your head. The orange glow falls around you and encases you in a beautiful bubble.

You have now grounded and protected your energy for the day. If at any point you feel as though your bubble has burst you can just close your eyes and imagine the bubble again. You could also imagine you are wearing a suit of armour or physically zipping yourself up from your feet to the top of your head.

Every day we come into contact with so many people and their energies. There are people known as 'energy vampires' who can literally suck the life out of you. You know that person who comes into your house, complains and gives you all of their woes and troubles? They leave practically dancing out of the door whilst you are left in a crumpled heap on the floor. This grounding and protecting can help you keep your energy vibrant and not feeling drained after your friend has left.

For the next week try grounding and protecting yourself. Keep a diary and see how you feel at the end of the week. If you normally just want to slump in front of the TV you may feel you have enough energy to do some yoga or go for a walk. Let me know how you get on.

Chakras

We talked earlier about auras. Each layer of your aura is interdependent with your chakras. Your chakras are another important part of your energetic being. Understanding when a chakra is wobbly can help you understand why you're feeling wobbly. Chakra is Sanskrit for spinning wheel. I describe them as spinning plates, like at a circus. When they are balanced the plates (chakras) spin perfectly. When they become unbalanced the plates (chakras) don't spin as smoothly.

Our chakras can become unbalanced for a variety of reasons. When a difficult situation occurs, such as a car crash, there are lots of emotions going on for us: guilt, upset, anger. If we don't deal with these emotions they can cause our chakras to wobble and become imbalanced. If we continue to block our emotions and we still haven't dealt with them then it can cause us to sometimes feel it in the physical body. If we are dealing with stress on a daily basis and don't know how to manage it we can often feel it in the neck and shoulders or in the stomach. This stress can then lead to potential physical issues such as IBS or digestion issues.

Learning what your chakras are and how to balance them can help us in our day to day lives. It can help us to feel more in control of our emotions and bring awareness to our emotions too. Below is a guide of the seven major chakras within the human energy body.

Root Chakra: Located at the base of the spine and is the colour red. Physically it governs the kidneys, adrenals, hips, knees, lower back. Emotionally this chakra is all to do with security. Family, jobs, relationships. These are generally our very basic needs. If you are in danger of losing your house or your job this can easily knock your root chakra out of kilter. You can bring it back into balance by wearing red, carrying a red crystal and by taking time to meditate and ground yourself.

Sacral chakra: Located between the belly button and the top of the pubic bone, this chakra is orange in colour.

Physically it governs our reproductive organs. Emotionally it is to do with expressing ourselves creatively, self-esteem, intimacy and sexuality.

Solar Plexus chakra: Located just under the ribcage in the centre of our bodies. This chakra is yellow in colour. Physically it governs the stomach, pancreas and liver. This chakra is like the main powerhouse for our bodies. It is where most of our energy comes from. Those suffering from chronic fatigue or MS can sometimes have an unbalanced solar plexus chakra. We can help to balance it by wearing yellow and carrying a piece of citrine or yellow jasper.

Heart chakra: Located at the centre of the chest. It is green in colour. Physically governs the heart, lungs and thymus gland. Emotionally it covers relationships, compassion and self-love. And not just relationships with others but the relationship with ourselves. And this relationship is the most important one in our lives. It took me a while to learn but if we aren't happy with the person we are, if we don't love ourselves fully, warts and all, how can we possibly love someone else? Wearing pink and greens can help to balance the heart chakra.

Throat Chakra: Located in the centre of the throat and blue in colour. The throat chakra governs communication. This chakra is connected with the heart chakra. If we don't love or respect ourselves then we can struggle to communicate in an honest and open way. If we don't express ourselves honestly, for fear of maybe offending others, it can lead to an unbalanced throat chakra. On the opposite end of the spectrum if we talk a lot and can't stop talking, but our words don't have actually any meaning behind them, this can also cause the throat chakra to be unbalanced. Wearing blues or placing a piece of sodalite on your throat can help.

Third eye chakra: Located on the forehead between the eyebrows, it is indigo in colour. Physically it governs the pituitary gland. Emotionally when balanced it helps with opening up psychically and clear vision. When unbalanced it can cause headaches, nightmares and difficulty concentrating.

Crown chakra: Located above the head and is white or gold in colour. Physically it governs the pineal gland. Emotionally it is to do with spirit connection, wisdom and knowledge. When unbalanced it can lead to materialism, spiritual addiction and apathy.

So how does it help you to know about your chakras? Understanding where the different chakras are and what they govern physically and emotionally can make us more aware of what's going on for us and why we feel a certain way. If one chakra becomes imbalanced it can have a knock-on effect for our other chakras. When our chakras are all spinning perfectly we become free of stress, relaxed and have a sense of inner calm.

You can do chakra meditations to help bring them into balance. You can also place crystals of corresponding colours along the main chakras in the body.

As a final note, I should say that as well as there being seven major chakras there are 22 minor ones. I'm not going to go into the minor ones here as I feel gaining a good grasp on the seven major ones first will give you a solid foundation to move forward.

Reiki

What does Reiki have to do with energy and chakras then? A lot! Reiki is a type of energy healing. It can be used to help balance a person's chakras. Reiki is a Japanese word. It is usually translated as 'universal energy' or 'life force energy'. Rei is translated as the 'wisdom and knowledge of the entire Universe' and Ki is the 'life-force energy which flows through every living thing- plants, animals, and people'.

This is the Japanese Kanji for Reiki:

So where does Reiki come from?

Mikao Usui was born on 15 August 1865 in Japan. He was a highly educated man, who spoke several languages and was very knowledgeable in medicine, philosophy and theology. He is believed to have studied Japanese and Chinese healing techniques. He studied spirituality in his spare time. Whilst on a retreat on Mount Kurama he had an unusual experience which changed his life. One morning he noticed a light in the dark sky. It seemed to be moving rapidly towards him. He decided to remain seated. As the light came closer it seemed to hit his forehead. He began to see strange symbols appearing before his eyes. He became aware of information being imparted to him as each symbol came into view. He knew he had received insight into a powerful healing method.

Dr Usui then went on to develop this healing and in 1921 opened his own clinic and began to teach Reiki for the first time. In 1925 a man named Dr Hayashi became a student of Dr Usui. Dr Usui died 9 months later. Hayashi stayed at the school until 1931. It was through Dr Hayashi that Reiki came to the west. He had treated a lady named Mrs Takata, who was so impressed with the treatment she wanted to become a practitioner herself. She lived in Hawaii and initiated 22 teachers. There are now thousands of Reiki practitioners worldwide who all practice Usui Reiki or a variation of this.

What are the benefits of Reiki?

Reiki treatments help the body to reach a state of relaxation. When the body is relaxed it triggers the body's natural healing abilities and improves and maintains health. There are numerous benefits of Reiki and the list is endless. Some of these include:

- Reducing stress and aiding relaxation
- Supporting the body's natural ability to heal
- Providing a feeling of calmness and serenity
- Aiding better sleep
- Restoring the body's natural energies
- Helping relieve aches and pains
- Dissolving energy blockages in the body
- Increasing vitality
- Promoting a more positive outlook

Reiki has taught me the importance of working with energy. What I like about it is that you learn it then go away and as you work with it your style changes and you adapt.

What should you expect from a therapy?

Reiki is a hands on/hands off therapy. The Reiki therapist channels the universal energy through their hands. People also feel different things during a Reiki session. Like I said earlier we are all unique so therefore our experiences will be unique. Some people feel heat, some cold and some tingling. You lie down on a couch fully clothed and the Reiki therapist will work with your energy field. Treatments normally last around 35-45 minutes. Again, this depends on the therapist and how much healing you need.

How will you feel after that?

Most people say they feel calmer, more relaxed and less stressed; however, I always recommend keeping a journal. This way you will see how Reiki has benefited you. Remember it works on your emotions and energy as well as the physical. If physically you aren't in pain it can help your emotions. Because we don't see these then sometimes we dismiss it as not working. Keep an open mind.

You can train in Reiki Level 1 to work with Reiki on yourself and your loved ones. Reiki Level 2 is if you want to become a practitioner. Reiki Level 3 is Master level where the energies become stronger and then there is teacher level. It is such a simple therapy to learn and can help you to build your intuition and learn to work with energy. Try it! You can find Reiki therapists across the world. If you look at the Reiki Federation website there are Reiki practitioners across the UK, both offering treatments and training. If you try it let me know how you get on #AGentlehugforthesoul

Access Bars

I had my first Access Bars taster session in January 2016. I had no idea what it was. I had never heard of it so didn't know what to expect. This chap placed his fingers on my head, feet, and hands and back to different points on my head. I walked away and thought it was a bit like my first

Reiki session. I didn't feel anything. I went home and set my first boundary to my ex. "Wow, that was powerful!" I thought - where did that come from?

Later that year I encountered Access Bars again. I asked the practitioner how she described it to people. She said it's like sucking all the crap and negativity out of your mind. It's also been described to me as like resetting the hard drive on the computer.

In 2017 I learned how to offer Access Bars as a treatment; I was the only student that day and it was amazing! Rachael gave me a treatment first, and then I gave her one. It was very hands on and practical. When she was placing her hands on different points on my head I could feel the energy in different places in my body. I could hear, like a radio being tuned in in my ear, and it was saying, "Really bad for you" so I kept repeating the words until I could laugh at them. I clearly saw the word 'Labels' written on a blackboard. Underneath the word this little guy wrote 'The Protector', 'The Enabler', 'The Fixer'. He then wiped those words off and replaced them with the words 'I Am Loving, Loyal, Joyful'. For most of my life I had viewed myself as a protector and fixer of people. I thought wrongly that I could save people.

Later on, in my treatment, the word 'Expectations' was written up and wiped off the blackboard. It was replaced with the word 'Values'. What values do I have and what values would I like other people to have? 'Respect. Loyalty. Honesty'.

I saw mermaids, unicorns and dragons. Just because you don't see it doesn't mean it isn't real.

I then gave Rachael a treatment. Rachael asked what else I was holding on to as she could feel tension in my belly and there was something there. She asked me to sit with it. It was an ugly devil. I couldn't talk to it or look at it, as it was so ugly. She asked me to ask what it wanted. It said it just wanted to be loved. I ended up giving it a cuddle and cradling it like a new-born baby. I think after everything with my ex there was a piece of me that felt unloved. I thought I wouldn't treat a stranger like this so why am I treating myself like it. I cried and my teacher cried. It felt like a huge release.

Access Bars is not something you can work on yourself so I highly recommend that you seek out a practitioner. There are practitioners worldwide so whether you live in Texas or Timbuktu there should be someone nearby. You can find more information at the end of this book with useful websites. With this type of treatment, they say the worst-case scenario is it feels like a gentle head massage; in the best case it can change your life. For me it was the latter – it was the first time I was able to love myself fully. If you have had a treatment let me know what you thought! #AGentlehugforthesoul

Crystals

I love working with crystals. I have them all around my house and pick them for different situations and depending how I feel on the day. The word crystal comes from krystallos (clear ice in Ancient Greek). Crystals take millions of years to form and each one has its own vibrational energy. Crystals have been used for thousands of years. The ancient Egyptians used them for healing and teaching.

Crystals have gained in popularity over recent years. There was a 40% increase in google searches from crystals between 2014-2018. Celebrities such as Victoria Beckham, Adele and Gwyneth Paltrow swear by them.

Crystals are here to teach and serve us but their energy lies dormant until we awaken them. It is so easy to start working with crystals and gemstones. The main thing you should keep in mind is that 'intent is all'.

As each crystal is a living thing containing the universal life-force, it has its own higher self which links to Source. The higher self of each living thing in the natural world is known as a Deva. We can learn to connect to them and by doing this they are able to impart wisdom to us.

Devas are light beings, operating on a spiritual level through different forms of nature such as trees, flowers, rocks and stones. Their purpose is to balance the energy of the planet and show that we are all connected and interdependent. We need to link in with nature in order to survive.

Crystals are one of my favourite tools to work with. They are relatively inexpensive, easy to use and don't need much looking after. I bought my first crystal when I was 28. I was on a second date at a psychic evening down in Peterborough. At this particular evening there was a couple with three or four tables full of these beautiful stones. I had never heard of crystals before. I left my date sitting whilst I went to choose one. I was drawn to a rough chunk of pink stone, Rose Quartz. I bought it and put it in my bag. He went up and picked a stone too. We showed each other the crystals we had bought after the evening. We had both picked Rose quartz although his was in a Buddha shape. I took the crystal home and didn't really know what to do with it so I just went to bed holding it. It gave me such a warm feeling I always describe it now as a Gentle Hug for the Soul. I decided I wanted some more. At the time I had to drive 15 miles to the closest crystal shop and soon grew my collection.

When friends started to realise that I was interested in crystals they started asking me if I could get them this one or that one. I thought that I could maybe start buying them and selling. I started quite informally and later on set up a business. I didn't really know what I was doing back then but the more I worked with crystals the more I found them fascinating. I never knew that such small natural stones could help with such a variety of things.

Choosing a crystal

Sometimes crystals are gifted to you but sometimes you might want to choose your own. So how do you choose one? You can look at a selection and see if you are instinctively drawn to one. You can hold a few crystals, one at a time, in the palm of your hand and see which one feels good to you. You'll get a feeling, or in some way will know which crystal is the right one to choose. There is no wrong way to choose one. You will instinctively pick the one you need the most at that time.

I was in a meeting and the lady I was meeting showed me a crystal that she had picked at random that morning, without knowing its meaning. It was unakite. I told her it was for the heart chakra and was normally carried to ensure a healthy pregnancy. I asked her if she was pregnant and she confirmed she had recently done a test which was positive. So never doubt yourself. Intuitively you know what your body needs.

Cleansing your crystal

Your crystal can pick up negative energies so it's essential that when you first get a crystal home you cleanse it. There are various ways to do this. You can place your crystals in salt. Make sure you totally immerse them for 24 hours.

You can use water: just place them under running water. You can put them outside during a full moon and leave them overnight. Some people dig a hole and place them in the ground. Although, beware, I have heard of people not being able to find them again! Just check before you place them under water, as some crystals, such as selenite or malachite, can't be washed.

Programming your crystal

You have chosen your crystal, cleansed it and now you need to programme it. Programming gives the crystal a purpose linked with what you need. Hold the crystal in your left hand and ask that the crystal be programmed for healing or whatever else you need it to do. (If you're left handed place it in your right hand).

You can hold the crystal over your heart chakra and say something like 'I programme this crystal with love, to help and to heal.' Just do and say what feels right for you. Your crystal is now ready for you to work with.

My Top 10 crystals and their uses

1. Amethyst

Particularly effective in meditation and psychic work to develop clairvoyance and clairaudience. It can bring memories of past lives and worlds when placed on the third eye. Often called the all healer, it is one of the most effective crystals for any kind of healing work. Particularly helpful for addictions including those to alcohol and food. Amethyst can help to prevent insomnia. It soothes headaches if placed on the temples. It can soothe anger and impatience so is good to have in busy rooms e.g. kitchens or office. The Greeks believed it to be particularly effective against drunkenness. Wealthier Greeks and later the Romans would make wine goblets out of amethyst to guard against the excesses of wine. A stone of integrity, it was worn by Egyptian soldiers in battle so they wouldn't lose their courage in dangerous situations. In the Christian church amethyst was the gem of purity and is associated with bishops, who traditionally wear an amethyst ring.

2. Rose quartz

I describe this as a gentle hug for the soul. Everyone should have a piece of rose quartz! It is associated with the heart chakra and is the crystal of peace-making. Rose quartz is great for relationships, not only your relationships with others but with yourself too. You can't love anyone else until you love yourself. Essential for healers, it can help ease pain or tension, cuts or bruises and emotional wounds such as grief, stress, fear or anger. A rose quartz can help a girl through the early stages of blossoming womanhood as it is very good for increasing healthy self -love and self- esteem.

3. Citrine

A yellow stone for prosperity. Keep a piece in your purse to attract money in. It can help to release joy and brings spiritual powers into the everyday world. Regarded as the merchants' stone, citrine is famed for improving communication, increasing selling power and for attracting money or business. The citrine stone can be placed on the solar plexus chakra. It can help give us a much-needed boost of energy when needed.

4. Carnelian

Carnelian is an orange crystal of personal happiness and fulfilment. If you believe in your unique talents and follow your personal goals rather than those set by others you can achieve anything. It can relieve PMS and menopausal symptoms. It alleviates arthritis in men. It brings abundance in every way to home and family. Traditionally a protector against fire and storms, can be placed near entrances to the home, garage and on your desk to radiate positivity. It's also good for helping to rekindle lost passion in a relationship. Carnelian was used in Ancient Egyptian magic as protection for both the living and the dead. A carnelian was placed on the neck of the mummy to ensure the protection and rebirth of the spirit in the afterlife.

5. Smoky quartz

Smoky quartz is a black crystal. Known as a guardian against all forms of bad luck, it was traditionally made into crucifixes and set on bedroom walls to keep away evil. Excellent after a period of illness or depression for gently restoring energy and optimism. It helps to melt any energy blocks in the limbs, adrenal glands, pancreas and kidneys. It can aid meditation if you find concentration difficult. I have a piece next to my front and back door to stop negative energy coming into my home.

6. Malachite

Malachite is a beautiful swirly green crystal. Whereas I describe rose quartz as a gentle hug for the soul this one is like a sledgehammer to the heart. If you have deep routed heartache from childhood this allows those emotions to be released. Malachite is a cleansing and protective crystal for the industrialised world. It can help to cleanse the auric field and aids the heart, stomach, liver and lungs. I did my first crystal meditation with malachite before I knew what it was for and I cried. A lot. It helped to release some stuff I had been holding onto. In my meditation I saw the tin man. In the Wizard of Oz movie, the Tin Man is searching for his heart.

7. Selenite

This is a white/cloudy colour crystal. Selenite has the highest vibration of any crystal. For this reason, it is a great crystal to use to cleanse the aura. Place a piece in your living room on the window sill to absorb negative energy. It gently encourages all forms of communication. A powerful crystal of psychic communication. A stone that should be used by mediums and clairvoyants.

8. Lapis lazuli

A blue crystal with what looks like tiny gold flecks in it. It is associated with the brow chakra and helps to increase clairvoyant abilities. The ancient Egyptians regarded it as the stone of the gods. Partly because it reminded them of the starry heavens and also because it had medicinal properties that improve eyesight when powdered around the eyes. It can help to relieve headaches and migraines. It can calm the nervous system, reducing inflammation and pain. Around the home lapis can bring contentment and a strong sense of family loyalty.

9. Labradorite

I love this stone. It is black/ blue and shiny. Whenever you tilt it you can see different colours in it. It's helpful when it may be a good time to strike out alone, whether in business or to follow a private dream. It can help to strengthen the immune system and repair the aura. It can help to counter stress and psychological overdependence, whether on other people, medicines or food. It can help to bring creative dreams.

10. Clear quartz

The most common mineral on earth. A see-through, clear crystal, sometimes with patterns inside. Apparently, Hercules dropped the crystal of truth from Mount Olympus and it shattered into the millions of pieces that we find today as clear quartz crystal. The most versatile of all crystals and can be used for any healing, energising or cleansing work. Crystal clusters in the centre of a room help people to live and work together harmoniously. They can instil a sense of optimism and clear purpose and make others more receptive to innovation. It can help to absorb negativity from the atmosphere and transform it into rays of healing and positive feelings.

These are my top ten crystals from working with them over the past ten years. There are plenty more which I use depending on the circumstance. For example, blue chalcedony is also known as the speaker's stone so whenever I know I'm going to be giving a presentation I pop a piece in my pocket. Apache tears is a great one for anyone who is going through a time of bereavement. Aragonite sputnik is fabulous for placing next to TVs or computers to absorb EMF (electromotive force).

Crystal Water

Crystal water is water that has absorbed some of the crystal's energy. Crystal water can be simply made. A small crystal that has been cleansed can purify water of etheric pollution when placed in the bottom of a non-metallic container filled with tap water. Allow it to remain undisturbed for twelve hours. You could also place the water in natural sunlight if the container is glass.

When drunk, this crystal-clear water will have a wonderful cleansing effect on the bloodstream. Different crystals will have different effects. For example, rose quartz in a jug of water will infuse you with love. Shungite is a natural water filter. The Russians have been using this crystal for years and this is what Brita use in their water filters.

Crystal water bottles are a recent invention. These are simply water bottles with the crystal in the middle. Personally, I say save your money, make your own jug of crystal infused water and use a normal water bottle. You can use crystal water for cooking, making hot beverages, washing your hands and face and watering plants. Drinking crystal water is just a different way of using crystals in our everyday lives.

Now you have the lowdown on crystals I invite you to go and buy one. Please share and tell me which crystal you have bought. #AGentlehugforthesoul

Chapter 2: Gratitude and Mindfulness

Living in the present moment

So far, we have explored auras, chakras, Reiki, Access Bars and crystals. Another way of using energy is through our thoughts. What we think and what we say has a huge impact on our lives. Sometimes we may not even realise how important our thoughts are.

If you spend a great deal of time complaining and being negative then, guess what? You will attract other people who complain and are negative. When you say out loud 'I am always skint', your voice sends that vibration out into the universe. The universe hears you and goes 'yep you are always skint'.

Using the words, *I AM* is extremely powerful. I have realised over this last year that your thoughts can become reality. It can take time and patience but eventually by combining your thoughts with considered action you can get what you ask for.

For example, I wrote in my journal back in 2016 I want to write a book. Over the next year or so I kept writing that I wanted to write a book, it started off with me writing 'I want it to be a spiritual handbook' or something along those lines. Then I started to say it out loud to my close friends and family 'I want to write a book'. In November 2017 I went to the Mind Body Soul fair in Birmingham and spoke to a lovely chap who was selling some beautiful statues. I chose a person sitting in the lotus position as he/she looked so still and I was seeking stillness at that point.

He told me this when I bought it: "You have a monk with you. He is one of your guides. I can see him standing behind you whilst you're typing at a keyboard. I feel as though you're going to be writing a book. He will help you." This monk turned out to be called Budmit, who has helped me to write this book!

I'd never met this man before and how could he know I wanted to write a book? Now whether this was the push I needed or extra support I don't know. I placed a small picture on my vision board at the same time that said I would be a published author. At the beginning of 2018 I started telling people *I AM* going to write a book. It took another 3 months until those words became *I AM* writing a book. Finally, in April 2018 I sat down to write and wrote my first 5000 words in a day. The rest took a bit longer but it was the start I needed. Living in the present is huge. It is mindful. It is now. It is active. Try it. Live for today, not in the past or the present.

I AM

Life is not about doing. It's about being. To do is an active verb involving action. Often, many of us believe that to 'do' is beneficial. To do keeps our mind and body active. But we forget the To Be. The 'To Be' can still our mind and our bodies. Only when our minds and bodies are still can we think. When we are so busy doing we can become numb to the world around us, to our families, to our friends. We forget who we are.

When we are present and, in the moment, we remember who we actually are. We laugh. We cry. We feel sorrow. We feel happiness. We feel excitement. That is what our souls crave. To be and to feel. Be mindful. What does this mean? It means concentrating on what you are doing now. Not be thinking about yesterday or tomorrow. Not be thinking about all the chores that need doing or beating yourself up about a job you forgot to do yesterday. It's about watching your child on the swing and absorbing their laughter. Splashing about in the sea and really feeling the water on your skin. Watching a sunset or sunrise and being able to sit in that moment absorbing the rays. Walking barefoot on the grass or sand and thinking about the sensations on your feet. Appreciate the beauty that surrounds you. Walking down the street it may be a flower that you notice. A bird singing in the sky or a baby gurgling in a pushchair. The following was channelled by spirit.

The beauty in our life is everywhere. Once you start to notice it becomes apparent. The flowers. The trees. The birds. People. Colours. Notice. Notice the red of the poppies. The yellowness of the buttercups. The vibrancy of the purple buddleia. Acknowledge the fact that you have seen it and appreciate it. Sight is taken for granted. We absorb so much through our eyes without paying it attention. The more attention we pay the clearer things become.

They say beauty is in the eye of the beholder. It is. Depending on how you view the world will depend on how you view beauty. One person's view isn't necessarily another. Beauty isn't just an object or nature. It can be a sentiment or a gesture. Appreciate the beauty around and within.

Affirmations work because saying '*I AM*' talks about you in the present moment. It's not where you see yourself in five or ten years. It's about recognising you in that moment. I AM healthy. Yes, today you are healthy. If you say next week I will be healthy and you decide to eat a burger next week you will feel disappointed because you set an expectation for yourself that you would be healthy, and eating a burger and fries isn't seen as healthy.

Living in the present encourages mindfulness. It's about thinking who you are in this moment. Saying affirmations out loud gives those words a vibration. The words are carried out into the universe. It then creates what you have affirmed. Your thoughts contain energy so by stating how you are in the present and in this moment brings life to it.

To add extra life to your affirmations you have to try and feel it. If you are just starting to tell yourself 'I am beautiful' for example, how does that feel? Where do you feel beautiful? How does being a beautiful person feel? Or try, 'I am calm'. Where do you feel calm? What does calm feel like? Is it in the breath? The shoulders or the stomach? Take your time to experience your affirmations in your body as well as in your mind.

PRACTICAL TIP

Working with affirmations

You can buy affirmation cards and use these on a daily basis. A Google search will give you plenty of options.

You can write your own affirmations and stick these somewhere you will see them every day.

Say them out loud in the car, on the way to work, at work, whatever works for you

As part of a new moon ritual put 'I am' into my wishes to make them present

Which affirmation works best for you? Share them #AGentlehugforthesoul

Acceptance

God, grant me the serenity to accept the things I cannot change,

Courage to change the things I can,

And wisdom to know the difference

The Serenity Prayer by Reinhold Niebuhr

Acceptance can play a huge part in how you live your life. When something happens if your first thought is to resist it and not accept what's happening life feels much tougher. Acceptance and power go hand in hand. If you are in your own power it makes it so much easier to accept decisions and situations. Having a knowing that there is more to this life than meets the eye makes acceptance easier. Having an understanding that we are part of something bigger helps us find serenity.

Elisabeth Kubler Ross says that 'Our personal power is our inherent gift and our real strength'. I wish someone had told me this before the grand old age of 37!

We don't know how strong we are until we go through a tough time. When we worry about other people's opinions of us it can change how we act, what we do, what we say. We give our power away to others. At the end of the day when you are lying on your deathbed are you really going to give a crap about what your neighbour thinks of your house? Or that your friend thinks you're nuts because you use crystals? My dad thought I had joined a cult when I first started learning Reiki. Just because people think you are a bit different or a bit odd doesn't matter. Be happy with who you are instead of seeking to please others. Trying to please everyone else is mentally and emotionally exhausting. People will be happy in your company when they see how happy you are being YOU.

Owning your power

The following is a piece of channelled writing I did when I was looking for the words to write about power.

Sanctuary. Where is your sanctuary? At home? On holiday? In a field? By the sea? Where do you feel safe? There must be somewhere. To have a sanctuary is to have a space where you can be. Just be. No phones. No technology. Silence. Chatter. Human voices. Calm, inner sanctity. When you find your sanctuary nourish it. Keep it. BE in it. Just BE.......

Having a space to create, to adapt, to flourish. Within oneself. Is needed. To own yourself. To BE with yourself. To BE responsible for yourself. Do not let external thoughts in. Do not allow external people in. Allow only your thoughts in. Be they negative or positive, you own them. Allow and let go. You don't need these thoughts to go around and round in your head. Let them go. Thoughts, feelings, vibes are yours and yours alone. Even if someone has 'gotten into your head' you have allowed that. You have chosen to listen to their opinions and thoughts and let them become your own. Was it your thought or opinion in the first place? If not that's not yours. Don't own it. Don't allow it to filter through your brain and destroy you. It's not yours. Disown it.

I'm not saying that people aren't entitled to their opinions as they are. By all means seek advice when advice is wanted or needed. Just don't let their opinions become you. You are enough. You are plenty.

No-one can judge you. Well some people may try to but if they do their judgement is their 'stuff'. It's not yours. Don't allow other people's judgements to get in the way of a dream. Don't allow other people's judgements to cloud your mind. The judgements are theirs. Disown them.

What matters? YOU. Form your own opinion on subjects and don't allow yourself to be swayed because someone else thinks you're wrong. Who are they to say you are?

PRACTICAL TIP

What can you do today to reclaim your power? Don't wait until tomorrow or next week. What is it that you want to do TODAY?

Say NO if you don't want to do something and say YES to opportunities

You could try saying yes to an experience or event that you have always wanted to go along to but never have.

You could try saying no to that friend who always wants to chat about themselves but has no time or energy for you.

Do something that feels like playing to you: gardening, meditation, writing, have a water fight with the kids, phone a friend or relative you haven't spoken to in a while, bounce on a trampoline, paddle in a river, the sea or a paddling pool. PLAY and have fun without worrying what other people might think.

Gratitude

In Reiki we learn five precepts, which are:

- Just for Today, I will Not Worry
- Just for Today, I will Not be Angry
- Just for Today, I will be Grateful
- Just for Today, I will do my Work Honestly
- Just for Today, I will be Kind to Every Living Thing

It was an introduction for me into mindfulness and gratitude. The 'Just for Today' part teaches us to live in the present. Not to think about the past or the future but to be here, now, in the moment. The second parts are simple reminders of how to live our lives. There is no point in worrying about what may come in the future, it's a waste of our time and energy.

Trying to remain calm in all situations can be difficult. Being angry every day for no reason can cause us to become unwell, to have a feeling of stuckness. Let go of any anger you feel from your past as it won't serve you today. All it will do is eat you up and make you feel ill.

Be grateful. Even though I learnt this nearly ten years ago it's only really the last year or so that I have been practising gratefulness or gratitude. I remember sitting on a beach last summer whilst my two kids were paddling in the sea. I was so grateful for that moment. For being able to watch my children playing. To be able to hear their laughter in the air. To be able to hold them in my arms and hug them. I was grateful for the sunshine. For the beautiful sea and sand. It was a real turning point for me as it was the first time I had taken the kids to the beach alone, knowing we wouldn't be doing this with their dad again as a family. We had just moved into our new house and I felt free. It was such a liberating feeling and I sat there thanking everything and everyone who had made this possible.

Being grateful can really help our mindset. In May 2018, my three-year-old daughter fell off the slide. I was in the kitchen cooking and just heard this blood curdling scream. She couldn't tell me what was wrong then I realised my hands were covered in blood. I rang 999 and pressed a cloth on the back of her head. The ambulance arrived in about 5 minutes. They said they thought it looked OK but as a precaution they would take us to hospital. My daughter was beside herself. My neighbour had just got back from doing the school run with her grandchildren so she said she would look after my eldest son. I grabbed my bag, washed the blood off my hands and went to the hospital. The ambulance man was very kind and reassuring. They were all lovely to me and my daughter. We had a two-hour wait in the hospital. I hadn't packed any food so we ate popcorn and crisps from the vending machine. We were finally called through and the lovely nurse, Kate, cleaned my daughter's hair and got another nurse to come and help her put some glue in it. It looked like a huge split in her head bless her! We returned home and picked up my son from my neighbour's house.

Why am I telling you this story?

Whilst I was at the hospital I asked my neighbour to look through the window and check I had switched the oven off as I had dashed out. She said everything looked OK.

When I returned to my home 3 hours after I had left I had switched the hob off but left a garlic bread in the oven, which was black. The house had that burnt smell but there wasn't any smoke.

I am grateful in this situation that:

- my daughter wasn't knocked unconscious and her head can heal
- people moved over and made way for the ambulance to get through
- for the kindness and compassion of the ambulance drivers
- for the patience of my daughter in the waiting room
- for the vending machines that provided us with snacks I had forgotten to pack
- for the trained staff who knew how to fix my daughter's head
- for the lovely lady taxi driver who brought us home
- for my neighbour who looked after my son
- finally, even though my garlic bread was completely burnt to a crisp, that I didn't have a fire in my home and lose all of our memories

It is easy when we are locked in a situation to struggle to find anything to be grateful for. It's only when we step back from the chaos of a situation that we can think, 'OK this shit might be going on but you know what, I'm grateful for my friends' or I'm grateful for my children'. If you are feeling alone it might be that you are grateful for your breath or your home.

You can do gratitude exercises in the morning or in an evening. I often run through my gratitude list in the morning. Before I even get out of bed I say I am thankful for my children, my bed, my family, the sunshine, my body, my house, my life, my friends and I really mean it. I truly am grateful for what I have in my life and being alive.

Sometimes my kids and I do a gratitude walk where we take it in turns to say what we are thankful for. The kids aren't always on board with this! Some people write down what they are grateful for.

Do whatever works for you. By saying 'thank you' and being grateful for what you have allows space for more to come.

PRACTICAL TIP

Working with gratitude

Keep a Gratitude journal - what are you thankful for? Aim to write down three things each day.

Do a gratitude walk - what are you thankful for?

Write down just one thing you are grateful for today and pop the slip of paper in a jar. At the end of the year read them. This will make you realise how much you have in your life to be grateful for.

Feel free to share what you are grateful for with #AGentlehugforthesoul

Working with worry and fear

I used to work at a retail superstore, which was a 45-minute drive from my home. One particularly icy morning I woke up and asked my ex what should I do if I skidded on the ice. He told me. I was driving down a single lane road when I skidded. I completely forgot what he had told me. The car behind me swerved and crashed into the side of me. I had no idea what to do, as I'd never crashed before. I wasn't thinking straight, was cold and a bit panicky. The lady who had crashed into me drove off before the police arrived. I hadn't taken her details or car registration. Luckily, I was fine but my car was a write off and I later found out that it was a CAT D which meant it wasn't actually insured! I chose to drive another way to work after that and one day a van in front of me indicated left, as I went to overtake him on the right he suddenly swung right and forced me off the road into a tree. I was OK but the car wasn't.

These two crashes happened within a space of six months. Whilst on my honeymoon in November 2010 I had heard that the weather was really bad back home and I was panicking about driving to work. Seriously who thinks about driving to work when you're on honeymoon in the Maldives! As I was lying down having a massage I just saw the words in my mind 'Fear Not the Unknown' This has stuck with me ever since.

We don't know what is around the corner. We don't know what is going to happen tomorrow or next week. So why spend our precious time that we have worrying about things that haven't manifested yet!

Worrying and living in a state of fear is a waste of our time and energy. If you are worrying about what may happen in five- or ten-years' time you are not living in the I Am, the present. Tomorrow your life could change in a way you didn't plan or prepare for. I love living in the I AM, the only downside is that I am more likely to appear disorganised and last minute.

The next time a worry or fear enters your mind write it down on a post it or a piece of paper. Leave it then go back an hour later and read it. Are you still worried or fearful about it? If so write down the reasons why. Is it because you have been told since you were a child that you can't do this particular thing? Is it because you have some limiting beliefs you need to work through? Once you begin to identify the CAUSE of your worry or fear then you can find a SOLUTION to it.

Let's break down my earlier example

1. It was an icy day and I had never driven on the ice before. I didn't know what to do if my car skidded on ice.

2. I created fear and worry of skidding on ice. The energy of fear and worry went out into the Universe.

3. I ended up skidding and crashing my car

4. I then continued to worry that the same thing would happen again. Why? Because it had happened before. The chances of it happening again were, in reality, extremely slim.

5. Hearing the words Fear Not The Unknown made me realise that whilst I was in a beautiful place where I was supposed to be in the moment and enjoying my holiday I was too busy worrying about the POSSIBILITY of another crash to fully appreciate the moment.

When you have got to the cause of your worry or fear write down the words FEAR NOT THE UNKNOWN on a piece of paper and place it somewhere you will see it every day.

When we begin to live without fear and without worry we begin to live in the present. When we live in the present we are more likely to grasp opportunities that come our way. To say yes to events. To say yes to doing something that might be outside of your comfort zone.

This is how we grow as people. We say yes to something we haven't done before. I'm not talking about doing anything illegal or that can put you or others at risk, but I am inviting you to say yes to going on that skydive you always wanted to do. Say yes to a new job opportunity. Just ask your boss if you can speak to them about a pay rise. They might say no BUT you asked! You got off your comfy chair and did something because you weren't afraid of the consequences. When we do this our lives start to open up.

When I first started writing about the comfort zone I thought I've never stepped out of my comfort zone, but looking back I realised that actually I do it quite a lot. From sailing on a ship at 15 to teaching English in Mexico at 19; from jumping off a yacht in Hong Kong despite a fear of drowning to doing my first Facebook live.

I was nominated for Independent Business of the Year at the Yorkshire Choice Awards in 2017. My friend, Lisa, couldn't come as she had had bereavement in the family. I thought I'll just go by myself. There were probably around a thousand people at this event. I put on a long black dress, bought myself a new pair of earrings and headed off in a taxi by myself. I had never been anywhere like this before. I knew one person in the room - I say 'knew', I didn't really! I had seen him on stage giving an inspirational talk in early 2017. His name is Richard McCann. If you get a chance to go and see him I highly recommend you do.

I walked into this huge room, grabbed a glass of champagne and Richard was one of the first people that I saw. I went up to him, he was in the middle of a conversation so I sort of hovered around the edges then said, "Hi, I saw you here, then bumped into you and talked to you!" He obviously had no idea who I was but it didn't matter. We chatted for a short while then I bumped into a lady I followed on Facebook who does some inspirational work with women. Then I sat on a table with 12 strangers and talked. I felt uncomfortable for the first 3 minutes when I walked in the room. The other 3 hours I was absolutely fine.

Just because you haven't done something before doesn't mean you can't do it. In order for us to grow as human beings we need to expand our thinking, our experiences, our lives.

What can you do to take yourself out of your comfort zone? Here are some of the ways I've stretched mine:

- Snorkelling: I have a fear of deep water and I can't use those snorkel masks at all, I just don't get the breathing thing. I used the eye mask and just kept holding my breath then coming up for air.

- When I went to the Richard McCann I Can workshop he pushed me out of my comfort zone by asking me to text 3 people closest to me and ask them what they liked about me. I asked my mam, dad and sister. I had never asked them before.

- Joining a networking group in January saying I would be happy to do a presentation and six weeks later there was a cancellation so I was asked if I could do it. I said yes. It was great: I enjoyed it and I got great feedback from the group.

- Doing my first Facebook Live – another experience that was nowhere near as bad as I thought. I made myself do it on my 37th birthday.

- Going on radio- I had emailed a local station and asked if I could talk about crystals and they said yes. As I was leaving the studio I just happened to say "I'm into loads of stuff: Angels, Tarot cards..." The DJ said, "Tarot cards? Can you come back next month and do me a reading on air?" Yes, a voice from somewhere inside me replied. Where did that come from? I've been on each month ever since to talk about a variety of topics.

So why do you want to push yourself out of your comfort zone?

Because if you don't take the opportunities that come your way, say yes and grab them with both hands you could potentially miss out on happiness, success and abundance. Say 'Yes' and if it's not right then somehow it will be cancelled or fall by the wayside. If it is right it will go ahead and you can carry on your journey. Stepping outside of your comfort zone makes you grow in a way you never thought possible. You walk away with your head held high thinking, "Yeah, man I did that."

What have you got to lose?

PRACTICAL TIP

Think of something that you have always wanted to do but never had the courage to go through with it.

Write it down in the present tense. For example, 'I am in a hot air balloon.' Picture yourself in the hot air balloon. How do you feel? Excited? Elated? Scared? If you do have a genuine fear of flying then I would suggest looking at overcoming that through hypnotherapy before you book onto your hot air balloon ride!

It could be something even simpler than this. For example, you could walk past a mum at school every day and smile hoping that she speaks to you. Write down, 'I am friends with x'. Then say hi first.

Start a conversation with a stranger. Go to the cinema to watch a movie by yourself. Making yourself do the small things makes it easier to do the big stuff.

SAY YES TO OPPORTUNITIES!

Share what you want to do! #AGentlehugforthesoul

Chapter 3: Love and Relationships

"There's power in love. Don't underestimate it. When you are loved and you know it. When you are cared for and you know it. When you love and you show it. It feels right. There's a reason for it and the reason is to do with Source. We were made by the power of love. Our lives are meant to be lived in love. Love your neighbour as yourself and while you're at it love yourself"

I absolutely loved watching Prince Harry and Meghan's wedding in the summer of 2018. Not because I'm a royalist but because it was something special. It brought people together. For me the icing on the cake was the Most Rev Bishop Michael Curry who spoke the words above I have quoted. What makes this quote universal across all religions is the word SOURCE. You can substitute it if you feel necessary with a particular God that you believe in and for those who don't believe in a particular God, I think SOURCE is a grand word!

Relationships can at times be hugely complex and seem immensely complicated. Why? Because we are here to learn and grow from each other.

Love the person, not the label

Every person in this world has a label on them. Be it son, daughter, mother, father, husband, wife. When you attach a label to a person you develop an expectation around them. The word 'mother', for example. What images does it conjure up for you? Someone who is homely? Someone who bakes cakes? What about a father? Someone strong that you can depend on? Someone who is great at DIY?

As a son or daughter your parents may have expectations of you. How you should behave. What you should wear. What job you should get.

Placing these expectations on people can cause disappointment. If someone doesn't live up to YOUR expectation it can cause friction. Removing these labels and actually thinking of the person for who they actually are makes life so much easier!

Love is everywhere. We feel love. We are love. Love isn't just between a husband and wife or parent and child. Love exists across boundaries. It precludes fear. Love can be a simple smile to a mum struggling with a crying baby. It can be felt between friends. Love is universal. You don't need to be religious or have any particular beliefs to love. Just be open to giving and receiving love. Some people, through life, can close themselves off to love. They may have felt hurt or pain and don't want to experience it again. Shutting ourselves off can actually cause more pain and hurt as we aren't open to receiving love from friends who want to support us, family who want to be close. Learning to love, give and receive is one of the greatest lessons we can learn. When we learn to give and receive. Open your heart.

When you look at someone for the person they are instead of the label you have given them it can make life so much easier.

Is there someone in your life that you have expectations of because of the label placed on them? Do you always feel disappointed that they aren't living up to their label? How can you start to see that person for the unique individual they are? Can you separate the label and the person?

Valuing friendships

Friendships are here for a reason, a season or a lifetime. That's what I remember hearing when I was in my twenties and I thought yes, that's so true and it has really helped me over the years to understand friendships and relationships.

I have a fabulous circle of friends who have been with me through various highs and lows. They may never know what I was like at school and we may not be able to reminisce about when I started primary school and I got smacked for not sitting on my chair but it doesn't matter. I feel as though I have finally found my tribe. This has taken me a while. I can probably count on one hand the number of friends from the past that I keep in regular contact with.

When you are young and at school the number of your friends and how popular you are may seem extremely important but as you get older you realise that yes, you can count on one hand the number of friends you have, BUT it doesn't matter. If you can tell your friends your deepest darkest secrets and they still like you, speak to you, and appreciate you then hang onto them for they are of great value.

You will have a variety of friendships over the years. Don't feel as though you have to keep being friends with someone if you don't have anything in common anymore or you just don't gel anymore. It doesn't make you a failure or a bad friend. It just means that it's time to move on and find your TRIBE. You will always have certain connections that keep in touch.

I did a meditation back in 2016 and the theme that entered my head was friends. This was my poem on the next page that I wrote following the meditation

Thank you for being a Friend

I can be Honest with You

Thank you for Listening

I can cry to you

Thank you for being there

For the laughter we share

Thank you, I appreciate

You taking Time

To spend time with Me

Chapter 4: Your Spiritual Army

Some of us are lucky enough in life that we have found our tribe; a support network of friends and family that are there for us through thick and thin, we can talk to them about our problems, worries and concerns. We can ask their advice and they freely give it. Often those friends and family have their own opinions, formed from their own experiences in life. Sometimes we just want to be able to talk to them without them actually offering advice, we sometimes just want them to listen. And sometimes it can feel as if we have no one.

You might not be able to see them but there are always people there for you. Your spiritual army. Your army is made up of a variety of beings. You may have loved ones who have passed into spirit. They've got your back. Everyone has a guardian angel; they have your back. Spirit guides, guess what? They have your back too. Oh, did I mention all the other types of angels? They have your back.

A friendly head's up though. Remember the Shy Bairns Get Nowt that I told you about earlier? The same applies with some members of your army. They like to be asked for help. This doesn't always need to be done out loud so if you're in a situation where you want to ask them for help and think I can't start saying 'Archangel... please can you help' in the middle of a crowded lift, just say it in your head. It works.

Your loved ones who have passed may make themselves known by feeling a gentle touch or a soft blow on your face.

Just because we can't always see them or hear them they are around. You can talk to any of them at any point. They will listen and try to help where possible. We all have free will but if we just need a bit extra support for something in our lives we have an army to call upon.

Spirit Guides

A spirit guide is someone who was once on this earth and now walks alongside you to help and uplift you. They are not necessarily family but someone from the past.

I didn't know about spirit guides until I had an Akashic Record reading in 2009. Not sure what Akashic Records are? Here is an explanation from the Edgar Cayce Association of Research and Enlightenment.

The Akashic Records, or 'The Book of Life' is akin to the hard drive on a computer. It stores every individual's information in it, who has ever lived on earth. The Akashic Records contain every single thing that has occurred in the history of the world. Be it a feeling, or a thought or even an intention.

An Akashic record is like a huge book. In this book is written all of the details of your life: what lessons you are meant to learn, who your spirit guides are, your personality, what soul group you belong to, what your life purpose is.

As part of my akashic reading I was told by the reader that he could see crystals and shells as part of my healing work. I was told that there would be communication prospects in my physical life. That I am very giving and wish to fulfil. He said that I was very sensitive and would be working in healing. I had this reading done back in 2009 when I hadn't even done my Reiki Level 2 practitioner course. I had bought a few crystals but had no idea back then of the healing powers they had and how I would come to use them.

As your family, society, life experiences, thoughts and beliefs through many lifetimes have shaped who you are today, you may not to be expressing who you truly are at a Soul level in your daily life. It can be difficult to be unbiased and neutral about yourself and even more difficult to clearly see any patterns or blocks present in your Record that are preventing you from expressing your Soul.

Sometimes we just need clarification that we are living authentically and aligned with the person we were born to be.

Why would you want an akashic record reading doing? I found it useful for providing insight. It was helpful knowledge I wasn't privy to at that time. It told me truths about myself that at that time I wasn't prepared to admit to. I'll be honest with you - when I first listened to my reading I cried. Why? Because here was this guy who had no idea who I was, who had never met me, telling me my deepest thoughts. He talked about a lack of confidence and how I was hiding my light under a bushel. Back then I didn't really know who I was or what I was doing with my life. I was working in retail and getting ready to get married. Looking back now I had no idea who I TRULY was.

From my Akashic record reading I found out I had 3 spirit guides. A Native American, a French girl and a lady from the Isle of Skye who worked with herbs.

Allana Simone lived in Paris between 1819-1847. She was a mathematics teacher and taught in an austere school. She immersed herself in books. She died of consumption before her time. She is a strong willed, enigmatic character. She is a witness to my life. I'm very different to her. She holds my hand when needed. Using her hands there is a possibility of creative expression for me and sound is very good for me.

Pahdora was from the Isle of Skye. She helps align me to history and ancestry of the world. She was a white witch. She used to ground roots which she then used as medicinal aids. She would dig for crystals and understood the mineral content. She lived to 78 and was a small woman with an astute energy. Pahdora will work with me when using stones and crystals.

Arrowhead was a member of the Black Foot tribe in South of Montana. He ran everywhere and bonded with the earth. He had a high spiritual nature. He was always making things to ward off spirits. He has an earth energy and brings word of encouragement. The energies that walk with me are to do with media. I feel as though these spirit guides are with me at different times in my life.

In March 2017 I did a meditation to meet my spirit guide. I quite clearly saw a white horse, then a bit later a Native American. There are various meditations you can do to meet your spirit guide. I used to listen to one by Tony Stockwell every day for about 4 weeks. Towards the end of the 4th week was when my spirit guide finally appeared to me. Patience is key. They will make themselves known to you when the time is right. When he did appear, I was a bit shocked. I asked him what I was here to do. His answer? To teach. To teach what I asked? He just laughed! Thanks, I thought.

If you are striving to meet your spirit guide just be aware that when you do finally meet them they may not always provide the answers you are looking for. You have to work at it. They only appear when you are ready. One of my clients had been telling me that she was getting frustrated as she wanted to meet her spirit guide. She said she had been telling them off. Whilst I was giving her a treatment I saw in my mind's eye a man. I had no idea who he was so I asked in my head, "Are you for me or my client?"

"Your client", he replied. He was wearing a turban and a white smock. He was in the desert and was sat on a horse. He felt like a gentle man who was passionate about his cause and led his men into battle. I felt the same qualities resonated in my client. Her spirit guide had come through to me instead of to her. Different guides appear to us at different times in our lives when needed. Your guides will bring you great blessings and spiritual strength.

The monk I spoke about earlier who came through at the Mind Body Spirit fair in Birmingham has since appeared to me in meditations. Again, it took a while. The first time he was in the distance wearing a hood so I couldn't see his face. All I got was the word Tibet. The second time he whipped his hood down so I could see his face. He then took me to a very grand temple in Tibet, which he told me had been donated to the monks by a very wealthy landowner, which was why it was full of gold and really grand, ornate ornaments. The last time he took me to a small door at the back of the temple, which led to a small, grey, bare room. One monk was sitting in it. I said, "It's so bare compared to the rest of the temple."

He replied "Sometimes we need to let go of everything around us and just go within."

I was so pleased to find out that I had these spirit guides in my life that I can talk to and who can advise me.

PRACTICAL TIP

How to connect to your spirit guide

The first thing you can do is just ask. Ask 'is my spirit guide currently present with me?' Do it when you aren't distracted by anything else. You may feel a shiver go through you, you may feel a blowing against your head. You might hear a voice or an image or song may appear to you.

Meditate: You can listen to guided meditations to begin with or start with a five-minute silent meditation and build yourself up to 20 minutes a day.

Angels

I became intrigued by angels after buying my first pack of angel cards in 2008. Did they exist? Are they real? I'd only every really heard or seen about angels in the Bible or those cherub statues you could buy at the garden centre then read Lorna Byrne's book *Angels in my Hair*. I was fascinated that this lady could talk to and see angels. Lorna explains in her book that everyone has a guardian angel. I strongly believe this. Knowing there is an angel assigned to every single person to be with them through their life brought me great comfort. You can't always see or hear them like you can your best friend. But know they are there.

I started talking to angels and asking them for help with various situations. I bought some more books and the more I read the more I was convinced that angels do exist. I discovered how angels can help you cut cords. With every person we meet in our lives we establish a connection. Sometimes that connection isn't always a good one. We can ask Archangel Michael to help cut the cords that attach us to others. Why would we want to cut cords? A person may latch onto us and physically drain us of energy. There may have been people in your past who were hurtful or abusive towards you. Remember earlier we spoke about negative energy? Well cutting cords is basically releasing another's negative energy from yours. Sometimes even though a person drains us we feel as though we need to keep going back. By cutting the cords and asking the angels to do this helps to disconnect your energy from theirs.

I did it a while ago when I first read about it. In 2017 whilst lying in the spare room one night I actually dreamt that Archangel Michael had cut the cords between me and my ex-husband. When I woke up I thanked Archangel Michael. One evening, again in the spare room, I was feeling really low and really upset about various issues between my ex and me. Before I went to sleep I said in my head that I just felt as if I needed a hug. Suddenly I felt a huge embrace before I drifted off to sleep. It made me feel safe, secure and loved.

I had a dream about Archangel Chamuel. I was driving along in a mini and pulled into a garage. I got out and looked up to see this person who must have been at least 8ft in front of me. You know when you see on a movie that someone looks at the bottom of their feet and all the way up. I said to him "Wow, you're big." He just smiled and shook my hand. When I asked his name, I heard Chamuel.

When I woke up this name kept going around and round in my head. I had an Encyclopaedia of Angels which I had bought but never read. I looked up Chamuel and found he was the Angel of Love. I strongly believe that angels exist to help us. We have free will and can choose what we want to do BUT if we need help and support you can call on the Angels to help and they will.

In September 2014 I was having a bit of a tough time. My husband wasn't working and I was seven months pregnant. I did a meditation. I saw a Gandalf like person with very blue eyes. When I asked him his name I got 'Gazriel'. I asked it again and got 'Azrael'. There is an Archangel Azrael. He helps to remove blocks from your spiritual path and hear the guidance of your spirit. My angel card that day was Forgiveness.

There are a number of angels with a variety of names and everyone has a guardian angel. You don't have to know which angel does which job in order to gain their help. If someone has been in a car crash or a serious accident people may speak of a stranger coming to help them who then disappeared. One of my students told me a story which I believe was definitely an angel visitor. My student was 19 and had been taken into a hospital when she was 26 weeks pregnant. When she arrived, she was told that her baby would die and she was very ill. As she lay in bed crying a black nurse came along and spoke to her. Why are you crying she asked? Because I'm going to lose my baby. "Have faith" this nurse replied and walked off. The next day when my student asked about this nurse she was told that there were no black nurses on the ward or in the neighbouring wards. So where did she come from? My student's baby survived.

PRACTICAL TIPS

Next time you are driving somewhere that you know is going to be busy do this. Before you set off in your car ask the angels to find you a space as close as possible to the entrance. It's that simple. If it works the first time and you don't believe it try it again and again until you ALWAYS find a space. I am rubbish with directions and always get lost when driving even with sat nav on. However, I have noticed that if I ask the angels to make sure I don't get lost before I go somewhere a car ALWAYS pulls out of the junction where I need to turn.

Secondly ask the Angels to show you a sign that they are with you. It may not happen straight away and generally the angel won't suddenly appear in front of you but just take notice of what you find through the day. For example, feathers. White feathers often show up as a sign that angels are nearby. You might spot a shape in the cloud which is angel shaped. By asking for proof and receiving a sign this helps you to ask for bigger issues.

You might find that when you start reading about angels you meet someone who does angel cards, or you speak to someone who tells you to read another book on Angels. Once you start exploring this theme they have a habit of keeping you on track.

If you feel as though there is a relationship you have with a person and this relationship is draining you and serving you no purpose you can ask Archangel Michael to cut the cords between you and that person. All you have to do is close your eyes and take a few deep breaths. Now think of the person you would like to cut the cords with. Ask Archangel Michael to come close. Ask him to please use his sword to cut any cords that are no longer necessary between you and that person. When you feel as if it is done, or you can visualise it thank Archangel Michael for his help.

Just a note. Sometimes this exercise can be extremely liberating especially when doing with people in the past. I feel if it is done in the present it can be more difficult. Like I said earlier we are here to learn lessons from people in order to grow. If we haven't learnt those lessons from that particular person the cords can't always be cut.

Angel cards and tarot cards

When I went to see a medium for the first time she told me that she could see angel cards in my life. I had no idea at that time what they were. When I got home I Googled them and bought a pack of Doreen Virtue's angel cards.

Angel cards can help you in your daily life. They provide messages of support when we feel at our lowest. They can provide guidance in your life. I have been working with angel cards now for nearly ten years and they are always right. Sometimes a card doesn't seem relevant. However, if we reflect on it at the end of the day or the week we often find it does make sense. I now use three different packs and choose one from each pack to see what is coming in the week ahead.

Tarot cards can be used in a similar way. You can take one for the day and see what it means. I tend to use tarot more for certain situations or to look more deeply when I have a question about something that is going on for me or for my business. Sometimes the tarot can show us aspects of ourselves that we may not feel willing to address as we aren't in the right place emotionally. I couldn't touch my tarot cards for most of the time whilst I was going through my separation because I felt too emotional and vulnerable. And it didn't feel right.

Both types of cards can help us to really get in tune with who we are, with our emotions, how we are feeling, what's going on for us and how to handle these emotions too.

PRACTICAL TIP

Choosing and working with your cards

There's a huge selection of cards out there. You have to choose what's right for you. Which ones are you drawn to? Which pictures? There isn't a right or wrong pack. When you first get them home make sure you separate each card as sometimes they can stick together. Some people like to smudge them to cleanse them of any negative energy. Some people place them in a special bag rather than in a box. It all depends on what you feel like doing.

Shuffle them and ask in your head or aloud which card do I need the most today. And keep shuffling until you feel as though you need to stop. Sometimes the card surprises me and sometimes I'm like yep that's definitely the one for me. Keeping a diary can help you understand the meaning of the card for you.

Using cards can help to bring you in line with your emotions and increase your intuition as you reflect on the messages they share. They can help to support and guide you in your life.

Angel Numbers

Angels can often try to connect with us through numbers. Have you ever been through a period in your life where you keep looking at the clock and seeing 11:11 or 3:33? Back in 2014 my ex and I were watching an episode of a TV show called 19:19. Later that night my son woke up with an awful cough, he couldn't catch his breath, was shaking and panicking. We called an ambulance as we weren't sure what was happening. We found out it was croup. The ambulance registration had 1919 as part of it. When I googled 1919 I found it was an Angel number and found that the number

1 is all about new beginnings and the number 9 is all about service to others, leadership and leading others by positive example. This happened a few weeks before my daughter was born, which I took as new beginnings. The number 9 was a reminder that my work was to be of service to others.

This hasn't been the only time numbers have been significant in my life. I went on a date with Chris. After meeting him for the first time I was driving home and stopped at a set of traffic lights. I looked down at my dashboard and had to quickly grab my camera to take a photo as I thought no one will believe me. It showed 11 degrees, 11:11am, 111 miles left in my tank. Seriously! The number 1 is all about new beginnings.

If you keep seeing the same numbers everywhere the angels are trying to tell you something. These are what the angel numbers generally mean:

Angel Number 1 is all about new beginnings, opportunities and projects. Having a positive and optimistic attitude. Take positive steps forward to achieve your goals. Your angels want you to achieve them. Don't allow fears, doubts or concerns to hold you back from living and serving your Divine life purpose and soul mission.

Angel Number 2 is a message to display compassion, diplomacy, consideration and adaptability as you passionately serve others in your day to day life. Trust in the divine and follow your life purpose.

Angel Number 3 is an indication that your angels are trying to get your attention. Follow your intuition and inner-wisdom. Take action Manifest your desires using your creative skills. Be optimistic and enthusiastic in pursuing your life goal.

Angel Number 4 is a sign that angels are offering you love, support, encouragement and inner-strength. Take positive action towards your highest intentions, aspirations and goals, the Universe works in your favour and helps you to establish solid foundations and advance you along your path.

Angel Number 5 is a sign that important life changes are on their way. These changes will bring about many positive opportunities for you. Look upon these changes with an optimistic and positive attitude as they are destined to bring you many long-term benefits. Remember to be grateful for what comes your way.

Angel Number 6 brings a message from the angels to keep a balance between your material life and your spiritual one. Take responsibility for your own life and be honest in all of your dealings. Be grateful for what you have already, as an attitude of gratitude encourages further positive abundance into your life.

Angel Number 7 is a sign that obstacles have been overcome and successes have been realized. Your angels are happy with your life choices. They are telling you that you are currently on the right path. You are encouraged to keep up the good work you have been doing as you are successfully serving your soul purpose and your angels are supporting you all the way. Positive things will flow freely towards you, and this will assist you in your journey.

Angel Number 8 is a positive sign of encouragement from your angels telling of achievements, success, moving forward and progress. Stay optimistic and listen to your intuition and inner-guidance Set solid foundations for yourself and your loved ones as this will ensure future prosperity.

Angel Number 9 is a sign from the angels that your life path and soul mission involve being of service to humanity through the use of your natural skills and talents. Angel Number 9 suggests that you are a natural lightworker and encourages you to look to ways to serve others in positively uplifting ways.

If there are certain numbers that you keep seeing in your life let me know! I'd love to see photos or hear your stories. #AGentlehugforthesoul.

In the next chapter I will be talking about death. Death is nothing to be feared. It is part of our life cycle. Inevitably with life comes death. However, if it is something you're uncomfortable with, feel free to skip it.

CHAPTER 5: Death and Past Lives

Death

I HAVE NEVER FEARED death or worried about it. I believe there is something afterwards and it's not the end. My first close experience of death was Christmas Day 1999. My grandma, Florence Banks, had been ill for a while. The doctors had allowed her out of the hospital and home for Christmas. On Christmas Eve the whole family went to wish her and my grandad a Merry Christmas. She was in bed and didn't appear to know what was going on. I think she hung on to make sure she saw everyone as she passed away in the early hours of Christmas Day morning. It was a really tough day and I remember my dad being extremely upset as it was his mam. I remember sitting in the funeral car and Macy Gray's tune 'I try to say goodbye', kept going around and around in my head. It's funny how songs have a habit of creeping into our minds at important points in our lives. My grandma was in her late seventies and had had a lovely life. With that knowledge comes an ACCEPTANCE. Death is inevitable but I think it is easier when you feel as though that person has experienced life. You have fond memories of them and it feels like that's the natural order.

My grandad, Arthur, AKA Monty, died only four months later. I was in Mexico at the time teaching English and flew back home for the funeral as I wanted to say goodbye.

My grandad on the train, Dennis, passed away in 2002. I was at Manchester Metropolitan university at the time waiting for a lecture to start when my dad rang to tell me. I cried on the bus all the way home, packed my bag and got the train home to Newcastle. He was also in his late seventies and had a good innings as they say. While these deaths were upsetting, I was able to accept them as I felt my grandparents had lived long and fulfilling lives.

Then in 2016 a very close friend of mine passed away. She was in her fifties. I met Lisa when I first got together with my ex, as she was his lodger. She'd had breast cancer years before I met her and survived it. Not long after Steve and I met we helped Lisa to find her own place. Lisa loved life: she loved going to the gym, socialising and swimming. We then set her up on an online dating site and she met Dave. A couple of weeks later she found out that the cancer had returned. Dave's late wife had passed fairly quickly from a brain tumour and she was worried about telling him but Dave was extremely supportive. Not long after they met they got engaged and they were married on September 11th 2011 (There's the numbers again: 9s and 1s.) She had never been married before and wasn't sure if she would make the actual wedding as she had been going through chemotherapy. She wore a wig and looked beautiful. She hated being the centre of attention so there were only six of us and my nine-month-old son. It was a beautiful wedding and a fabulous day.

We moved to York not long afterwards so I didn't see as much of her. Her cancer gradually spread over the next few years. She would ring me telling me how she was going to fight it and she wasn't scared. Then other days she would ring me crying as she was scared and all I could do was listen to her worries and fears and try to say comforting words.

Shortly before Lisa's death she rang me. She told me she loved me then rang off. I never said it back. She must have known she didn't have long left as she'd never told me she loved me before. I got a message from Dave a few days later to say that Lisa had been taken into hospital and he didn't think she had long left. I sent her a card telling her what a fabulous friend she had been, with a small rose quartz heart and a lavender pouch that I had made. I asked Dave to let Lisa know that I had sent them and to read the card to her. She died on October 24th 2016. My 36th birthday.

After Lisa's passing came the grief. I wasn't expecting it to hit the way it did. It was so raw, the pain, the hurt, the realisation I wouldn't see her again. I was trying to focus on the kids and be present but all I could feel was pain and loss.

The following Christmas I felt very low and isolated. My ex thought I might be depressed so asked me to go to the doctor. The doctor told me I wasn't depressed, just grieving but could refer myself for counselling if I felt I needed it. I called them but didn't feel as though I needed it. My friends had been extremely supportive and the more time I spent talking about Lisa the easier it became.

I share this story as a reminder that grief hurts. Losing a loved one is one of the most painful things we, as humans, can ever go through. There is no set time to recover from this loss. Sometimes the person can leave a huge void in us, in our hearts. Everyone processes grief differently and you need to allow yourself the time and space to do this.

If it means taking time out of your regular routine then do it. If it means you stay in bed crying all day do it. Grief is a lesson for us all. One thing that bonds us is that we all lose people we love. Yet we all deal with it differently. There is no set way to manage grief. Some of us may turn to drugs or alcohol to help numb our emotions. Some may go for counselling as they feel that talking about it will help. Some of us may bottle up our emotions as we are not used to talking about them. Having a great support network really helps.

PRACTICAL TIPS

Handling grief and loss

Allow yourself to fully feel the pain of grief, accept that it is a feeling and bereavement is a process.

Cry if you need to.

If you're angry tell people you're feeling angry that this person is no longer in your life.

Carry a piece of apache tears with you. I held this crystal constantly for about 3 months after Lisa passed away. It is a great crystal to help you go through the process of bereavement

Bereavement is a process to go through. If you are struggling then do ask for help from a professional. There is no need to go through this alone.

Talk to your friends and family; try not to bottle up your emotions.

Talk to a psychic if you would like to: I had a message from a psychic friend to say that Lisa was OK. She had been spending time around my children especially Eve as she'd always wanted a daughter. This brought me great comfort and I am sure that Lisa is always with us looking over us.

Past lives

I believe that as souls we have other lives to go into and we have lives that have passed before us. Lives that we may have lived before are known as past lives. Lives to be lived are future lives. There is a wealth of YouTube videos that can help you to access both past and future lives. Or you can visit a hypnotherapist to find out who you were before.

Some people, myself included, believe that your spirit has been here before. Your spirit returns to learn lessons it may not have had a chance to do in previous lives. You may be with members of your family and you may have lived together previously but with different relationships. You may have been reunited again in this life because they did something bad to you in a past life and they are here to make amends in this life, or you may have another karmic connection.

I believe that the spirit keeps returning until it is enlightened and has learnt the lessons it needs to. If you are going through a particularly tough patch in your life this is useful to remember. We decided to learn the lessons in this life before we came here. Knowing this helps us to take responsibility for our own lives.

Hypnosis can be used to guide you into a meditative state to remember who you were in a previous life. I was hypnotised in 2009. I lay on a treatment bed. She talked me into a meditative state. Then she asked me, "What are you wearing on your feet?" I thought, "You know what I've got on my feet, socks!" Then I realised that she was asking about my past life. Straight away I could see black boots.

She asked what else I was wearing. Red jodhpurs, a black jacket. I had a beard and this awful wiry black hair. I was a soldier. I was living in a small cottage in the woods with my wife and daughter. I felt as though it was my duty to serve the king and queen so I went off fighting. When I returned the enemy had burnt down the cottage where my family had been living. The hypnotist asked me where I was. The word 'Dordogne' appeared in my head. My geography isn't great and I never even knew that was an actual place! I was truly surprised when she told me it's in France! She asked me what I was meant to learn from that lifetime into this lifetime. I said I felt as though I had prioritised my work over my family in that life and I didn't need to do it again in this lifetime. That has been a valuable message for me as I make life decisions.

My son was five when he told me about his other mother. He said she was pretty. He talked about living in York before but that he didn't live in a house as big as this. His dad's name was Stephen and he had two sisters, Lucy and Madge. He told me he lived in London too. My daughter from the age of two kept talking about Meany and Tomas. She was obsessed with ballet. When she was about two and a half she asked me to do ballet with her. I tried doing what I thought were ballet poses only to be told, "That's not proper ballet mummy!"

When children first start to talk, listen carefully to what they say. Ask them questions and make notes for when they are older. Sometimes an imaginary friend may actually be a spirit with them. There are some fascinating cases out there of young children remembering past lives.

How does understanding about past lives help?

In the past life when I was the soldier I was working crazy long hours and rarely saw my family. I was working down in Peterborough and they were in Newcastle. I saw them maybe three or four times a year. Getting the message that essentially there is more to life than work was huge for me. Wisdom from past lives can make you look at your life from a different perspective. It can make you aware of any issues you have in relationships with certain people and potentially the reasons why. It can also help you focus on any lessons you are intended to learn in this lifetime.

In the next section we are going to look at spirits. If you think you have ever heard or seen one do let me know as I find this so fascinating.

Spirits

It wasn't until 2009 when I moved in with my ex-husband that I had my first encounters with spirits. The first night I slept there I woke up to hear a door banging. It was as if someone was trying to get into the house. I was lying in bed and slowly opened my eyes. As I woke up a bit more

I realised that someone was actually banging the en-suite door. I was so scared! I quickly turned over and as I did the sound stopped.

One afternoon I was lying on the settee trying to have an afternoon nap as I was on night shift that night. I couldn't sleep and out of the corner of my eye I saw a black shadow standing beside the door into the dining room. As I turned it flew at me before disappearing. One day I walked into the spare room to see the digital clock with the hours moving forward and the minutes going backwards. I wish now I'd filmed it.

I later found out that my ex had invited a priest round a couple of years previously as things had become so difficult. Gushes of wind had been felt on the stairs. You're probably thinking it must have been an old house. But it wasn't. It was a modern build. The first owner had only lived in it for six months before selling up at a loss! No wonder! Before the priest arrived all of the lightbulbs in the house smashed. When the priest did arrive, the doorbell rang out continuously. The spirits had been pressing the doorbell. When he came into the house to cleanse it he was confronted by the spirit of a man who told him to "Get off his drive". There were also the spirits of two children with him, a boy and girl. This man had abused both of his children. The priest managed to move the children on. He thought he had moved the man on too, but I think the spirit of this man stayed.

I have a couple of photos that show spirits. The first was taken at the York Castle Museum in the prison cell area. It shows clearly the back outline of the man. No-one would visit the Museum wearing a black suit like this. And his boots were like old work boots. The second photo was taken at Fountains Abbey in North Yorkshire. Again, it is so clear. A little monk boy praying. Fountains Abbey used to be a monastery years ago.

A friend of ours came to stay and she told us there was the spirit of a little girl in our house. Two weeks later another friend came to stay who told me there was the spirit of a little girl in our house who was there with an aunty-like figure. We were sat downstairs in the dining room when she was telling me this. There was no wind or breeze outside and we had the patio door open. When she mentioned the little girl, my son's football rolled along the path. We both looked and started laughing as we thought it was a sign from the little girl. My friend Lisa told me that the reason the aunty was there was to make sure the spirit of the girl was looked after. I told her we would look after her. My friend said she could see the aunty figure packing her bag. Her job was obviously done.

Having all of these ghostly experiences has made me aware of the afterlife – that there is something else after we pass. This helps us to understand that death isn't something to be afraid of. I have decided to share these experiences with you to normalise them, to help people have their own conversations about death and sprits without feeling like they're going crazy! We need to be able to talk about death to each other for our own wellbeing. Death cafes are places where people can meet to openly discuss death and losing their loved one. York ran its first ever Dead Good Festival in 2018 which again encouraged people to talk about the loss of their loved ones. Talking about it can make it less scary.

Spiritualist Churches and Circles

There are mediums and there are psychics. In a nutshell a medium is someone who connects with spirits and can get messages from loved ones for you. Psychics can see into the future.

When I lived in Peterborough I used to attend Jacqueline Lesley's monthly Psychic Fellowship evening. Jacqueline Lesley was the first medium I ever visited. On these evenings she would often have guest mediums. Even if I didn't get a message I would love listening to them for other people. I took it as extra validation that there was an afterlife. I remember one particular evening we had been asked to bring a flower or a picture of a flower in. I had taken this beautiful photo of some pink flowers and had put them in a frame so took those. I remember Jacqueline standing at the front and she picked up my frame. Straightaway she said, "I feel as though I'm with a very tall chap, very slim and his name is Johnny. Not John or Johnathan but Johnny. Can anyone take this?" I put my hand up. My grandma's brother was my Uncle Johnny. He was so tall, I remember him being bald, slim and tall. He would always wear a hat and was very polite. I wrote a poem to him when I was younger. She went on to tell me how he'd passed and how my dad and his family had scattered his ashes under a tree up in Ponteland, a place he liked to visit. I told her that was true. She went on to tell me that I would have a son, which I did. She could see us riding on a horse together along a beach. I was fascinated. I went along every month until my son was born.

We then moved to York and I discovered York Spiritualist Church. When my son finally started to sleep for a few hours I would escape to the church for a couple of hours' silence. When things weren't going well for me and my ex I would go there every Sunday looking for some comfort and reassurance. I was told several times by the mediums that it was the right thing. Now you might think they say that to everybody, but a medium at that church told me something incredibly specific. She asked me if my family had a connection with steam engines? It does. My great-great-granddad worked on the Railway line in Peterborough in the late 1800s. She asked me if someone had a picture of a red steam train in their house. It wasn't me, or my parents and I thought no more of it. Then two weeks later my parents came to visit. My 90-year-old grandma was moving from her home of seventy years to a flat and was getting rid of a load of stuff. My mam and dad had brought me some of her things.

In it was a 500-piece jigsaw of a red steam train that I had glued and framed for him when I was 16. I had completely forgotten about it. I still have it.

Going to the spiritualist church was a reminder that there is a bigger plan to life. It gave me confidence to go through with my divorce as I kept getting told you're making the right decision; you and your children will be fine. This year I decided to join an Open Circle. I had never been to one before and wasn't sure what to expect. We sat in a circle, around ten of us. The person leading the group did an opening prayer and then led us into meditation. Sometimes this meditation involved colours, chakras, picking gifts for others. Sometimes we work in a big group and we are asked to be given information from the spirit world Sometimes we do pair work such as tarot cards for each other or drawings. Sometimes we are guided into a meditation to connect with someone.

The first very clear person that I got was a young lad. He seemed to love travelling. I saw a purple angel then a flash to his mum who was very upset and he was trying to comfort her. I started feeling nauseous but wasn't sure why. When we came around the guy leading asked who wanted to go first, I offered. I described this young lad with a ponytail, that he seemed to like travelling and he was making me feel sick. The guy leading it said "Yes I can take that". I went on to describe the fact he wanted his mum to know he was OK. I said he's making me feel sick but I don't know why. "Go on" the guy said. I closed my eyes. "I feel as if he took his own life. But he didn't mean to?" Bingo! The guy told me he knew exactly whom I'd connected with. He was a very strong character, angry about a lot in his life so he got drunk and hanged himself, but he didn't mean to kill himself.

Attending open circles gives me a chance to connect with spirits who may want to come through to talk. It is practice for me to learn how to switch on and switch off spirit chatter. Some people can feel, hear and see spirits and have no idea how to control it. For me learning it in this environment has been extremely useful. When people pass to the spirit world and come through to communicate, they do so from a place of love. When you connect with spirit there are numerous benefits. If I have a decision to make I ask in my head and receive inner guidance. You never feel alone. When we face big losses in our life, either emotionally or materially, spirits are there to provide comfort and love. You trust yourself. You trust your decision-making processes.

PRACTICAL TIP

If you want to learn to develop your connection to spirit I suggest the following:

Head to a local spiritualist church, they often run open circles

Find a local Spiritual Development group or attend a weekend workshop

Connecting to spirit often takes practise and isn't something that can be achieved overnight

I believe it is well worth practising and investing time in

CHAPTER 6: Manifesting Your Dreams

WHEN YOU HAVE BEEN through a particularly stressful time at some point you do start to see the light at the end of the tunnel. It may only be a tiny chink but somewhere within you rises up this amazingly strong person. You decide now is the time to move on. To create the life that YOU want. Where do you start? Firstly, if you have been through an experience which has created a lack of self-esteem or self confidence in yourself I strongly suggest you work on that first. You need to believe in yourself and trust yourself. Remember YOU are amazing. YOU are strong. YOU are unique. YOU are fabulous. Whilst you are working on yourself you can also use the tools that I have written about below.

Vision boards

I had read for years about vision boards and how they could work but never committed to doing one. I did my first one after a holiday with my friend Lisa. We had discussed them on holiday and made a commitment to each other that we would make one each. As soon as I got home I decided to make my first vision board. I grabbed a load of Spirit and Destiny magazines and started cutting out images and phrases that meant something to me and that I wanted to attract into my lifwe.

I manifested a settee within 2 days. A friend contacted me and said she was clearing out her mum's house and did I want the purple Ikea bed settee? Yes please! That came off my noticeboard. The next thing was a camping trip. I had wanted to go camping for ages. Last year I wrote down that one of my goals was to go to Gaia Tribe. I placed the smallest photo in the world of a family camping. In May this year I took my kids to Gaia Tribe camping for the weekend.

There are still things on there to manifest and I trust they will, but sometimes they take time. I currently have on there a photo of New York, the Taj Mahal, a new car, a house... I said I wanted to be a published author and that is now reality! A friend of mine asked if he put a picture of a Lamborghini on there would it just appear. Unfortunately, not I said. When you look at your pictures you have to imagine yourself sitting in the Lamborghini. What does the interior smell like? What will the speedometer say? You have to believe that those dreams are within your grasp. He may end up with a Xmas gift where he can drive a Lamborghini for a day, you never know!

Vision boards work when you look at them every day. When you think about something you want it is an idea. When you write it down you give that idea energy. When you put a photo on a corkboard and look at it daily your brain begins to see that picture as real. When an opportunity then presents itself, you are more likely to say yes as you created that desire in the first place and it is foremost in your consciousness. I have known people to change their window screensavers to a particular car or holiday destination.

PRACTICAL TIP

How do you create a vision board?

Pinterest can give you endless ideas for designing your vision board. Here's my suggestion for a simple way to start. Buy a cork noticeboard.

I use cork as it's easier to change your pictures rather than cutting and sticking. Grab a pile of magazines and look through them. What words resonate with you?

What pictures do you want to put on your board? What symbolises your goals? Your dreams? Your desires? Where do you want to travel to? What do you want to see? Who do you want to work with? You can use these in business and in your personal life. Once you have filled your board with the quotes, houses, holiday destinations or experiences you desire, put it in a place where you will see it every day. Mine is on my kitchen unit and I look at it at least four or five times a day.

Vision boards work best when you are clear and focussed about what it is you want from your life. Dream BIG! Nothing is out of your reach! You are in charge of your destiny!

Share your vision board pictures at #AGentlehugforthesoul

We have the affirmation tool 'I AM' to put our goals into the present and we have a vision board where we can see our goals every day. Surely there is nothing else we can do to reach our goals is there? Yep, we can use the moon! "What?!" I hear you cry. Seriously.

If you think this is a load of tosh then feel free to skip the next bit but if you are passionate about achieving your goals and making your dreams reality then read on....

Working with the moon

I recently read Yasmin Boland's book, *Moonology*. I loved it and did my first full moon ritual. This was followed two weeks later by the new moon ritual. The new moon ritual is amazing. I sat down and wrote down my top 10 things I wanted to attract most into my life that month. Under these I wrote down the affirmation which would turn my want in the future into an *I AM* in the present. I then wrote down *how* I was going to achieve my want. I left it and didn't think much more about it.

I wasn't really sure if there was anything in this. One of my intentions had been to appear on TV or radio as a guest and talk about crystals or Reiki. Only two days later I had a phone call to ask me if I wanted to go on YO1 radio with June Tranmer, who runs the Healing Clinic in York. Unfortunately, as it was a breakfast show I couldn't get there due to doing the school run. But I emailed the station asking if they would like me to go on and talk about crystals. They said YES. By taking 30 minutes to set my new moon intentions I now have a monthly radio slot. I also manifested a guest appearance on a podcast. I did a Facebook Live and mentioned a lovely sales coach, Jules White. She acquired 10 new members in her Facebook Group that day. I messaged her telling her they were all from York and had heard about her from me. She thanked me. I asked her if I could appear as a guest on her podcast. She said yes. Having set my intentions, I then took the actions necessary to achieve my goals.

Working with the moon isn't just about setting wishes and desires. It is also about letting go and releasing. For the new and exciting stuff to come in we have to make space and this is where the Full Moon comes in.

On the evening of the Full Moon I write a list of anyone who has got my back up the month before - anyone who has annoyed me or irritated me. It can be family, friends, the bus driver who drove off without waiting for you, someone who barged past you without saying sorry. It can also be any habits or thought patterns that you don't want to hold onto anymore or that no longer serve you.

You write it all down, get it off your chest and then burn the list. By burning it, you are showing the universe that you aren't holding onto it any longer and releasing. I have been doing these full moon releases for about seven or eight months now. Just before one new moon I became extremely weepy and felt very fragile. I didn't particularly want to talk to anyone as I just wanted to cry. What was going on? After I spent a good hour sobbing I felt so much better and realised that actually even though I was doing this full moon work, my body also needed to release the stuff I was holding onto before the new moon so there would be space for my wishes. If you decide to start working with the new moon and full moon it's something to be aware of. There may be a physical release from within. Accept it and let it flow.

Nothing is out of your reach. As soon as we have an idea we can turn it into reality. It just requires a little bit of work. So how can you do it?

1. Have an idea
2. Write the idea down
3. Tell someone your idea
4. Tell someone that you are doing your idea
5. Create a vision board
6. Use the moon

'Shy bairns get nowt'. This is a Geordie phrase that I heard a lot of when I was growing up. If you don't ask for something you will never get it. The worst that can happen is someone says no. Then you find a way around it. Let me know how you get on working with the moon #AGentlehugforthesoul

FINAL THOUGHTS: Awakening and Walking Your Own Path

WHAT IS AN AWAKENING? It is becoming wise to yourself. It is acknowledging the greatness and vastness that is you. It is becoming aware. Becoming aware of you as a spirit being. Understanding that your spirit is within a physical body. Recognising sights and sounds and allowing your senses to fully embrace them. Living without ego. Recognising others for the wonderful spirit they are. Treating others with empathy and showing them understanding. More people are awakening as we transcend. We are in a very technological period of time. Whilst great for connecting us to potentially millions at the touch of a button, it can also lead to many feeling lonely or isolated. More so now than ever before, I feel. Searching externally for answers when instead we should be searching within, internally. Any answer you seek in terms of your life and your being are already inside. Sometimes we just need a bit of help finding tools to help us access that innerness.

I had my own awakening recently. Three of my Reiki students had mentioned the word 'awakening' to me but I had no real idea what it meant. It was August 2017 when I heard about awakening for the first time from my student, Keith. He had undergone what he called an awakening. He was talking to me about 5th dimensions and all this stuff I hadn't heard of before. My next student, Lizi, also talked of an awakening happening to her. I honestly didn't have a clue what she was talking about. She was very excited about it. I heard the word again at the York Healing Clinic. Awakenings seemed to be happening all around me!

It wasn't until I met Leanne in June 2018 that I got to experience this awakening for myself. Leanne came to learn Reiki Level 1 as she thought it might help her whilst developing her abilities as a medium. A few days after I met her I went on what I can only describe as a downer. I was extremely emotional, couldn't talk to my friends without crying, and had no idea what was going on with me. It lasted four days then on the Sunday I woke up and I felt fine: I was back to 'normal'. What was that about?

I then started waking up at 4.30am when my children were with their dad. And when I was waking up I couldn't get back to sleep so I was getting up, writing, watching webinars and meditating. I spoke to Leanne and she confirmed that this was an awakening. It's about moving from a 3rd dimension to a 5th dimension: operating as a collective consciousness. It's not about materialism and gain but living life to our truest and fullest purpose. Who says we have to work 9-5 in a dead end job we don't like?

I do believe we only go through this when we are ready. I don't think you can just make it happen. If something like this happens to you the best thing you can do is to accept and acknowledge it. Keep a journal. Write down how you feel. Meditate. There are loads of great meditations on YouTube. I particularly like listening to Steve Nobel who does transmissions from spirit. Jason Stephenson is also another guy whose meditations I enjoy.

Your passion is your purpose!

Go within. Find your passion, your inner flame. Light it. Work with it, not against it. We all have our calling, our path in life. Some people dream of being doctors, nurses or solicitors. Some people know from a young age what they want to do and where they are going. Be willing to dream. There are no boundaries to where life can take you except for those that you, your family, your friends or others around you put in place.

Walking a spiritual path sounds easy. It's not. Walking a spiritual path is challenging. It isn't all sweetness and light. People choosing this path haven't chosen it because it's an easy option. It has its forks and bends like anyone else's path.

2016 felt like a real journey of self-discovery for me. In terms of health, food, diet, family history, ancestral line, self-care. 2017 was a year for finding courage and inner strength and learning to be me again. 2018 has been another year of challenges and for putting my crazy inane trust into the Universe that everything was going to work out for the best. Who knows what the future will bring? But I know that I am tooled up and equipped to handle whatever life throws at me. If I fall, I will fall with grace. If I rise, I will rise with grace. Life is full of ups and downs and as long as we have what we need inside we will learn and grow stronger from it.

It took me 15 years to learn the various tools in my toolbox, which have provided me with a strong foundation for getting through some extremely challenging times. I would have loved to have known about these from childhood but we all learn at different times. Whether you have picked this book up at 18 or 88 it will be the right time for you to read it. Absorb it and let it be inside you. Even if you choose just one tool from this book that can serve you and support you in your day-to-day life this has been worthwhile. And that will make me extremely grateful that I have been able to help one person find another tool for their own spiritual toolbox. Life is a journey. Don't take life too seriously. Never question 'why me?'

We chose our path so let's walk it in the best way we can. I would like to leave you with a channelled message from spirit

In this Stillness. I lie. I breathe. I inhale. I exhale. I believe. I believe in me. I believe in you. Trust in me. Trust in you. Where there is stillness lies peace. Peace in your heart. Peace for you. Joy within. Joy without. I love me. I love you. Sounds of silence echo strong. Within. Without. No words. Breath. I inhale. I exhale.

10/7/2018

If you have enjoyed reading this book please leave a review on Amazon and share your book with a friend, share the love. Thank you.

About the Author

Lindsay Coldrick is a Spiritual Mentor, Access Bars Practitioner, Reiki Teacher and Crystal Healer. She also does Tarot and Angel cards. Lindsay is available for online work as well as 121 and teaching groups. Whether you are going through a particularly challenging time in your life or just feel stressed out on a daily basis, Lindsay can work with you.

Lindsay wrote this book as she doesn't want anyone to feel alone when they are going through a challenging time in their lives.

To connect with Lindsay, visit her website: www.nrghealing.co.uk or join the Facebook Group "A Gentle Hug for the Soul". Share your hashtags on Twitter and Instagram #AGentlehugforthesoul

Resources

- To find out more about Lorna Byrne check out www.lornabyrne.com
- To find out more about the moon check out Yasmin Boland www.yasminboland.com
- For bereavement check out www.cruse.org.uk
- Jacqueline Lesley http://jacquelinelesley.com
- Access Consciousness https://www.accessconsciousness.com/en
- UK Reiki Federation https://www.reikifed.co.uk/
- Spiritualist churches UK https://www.thespiritualist.org/
- York Spiritualist Church https://www.yorkspiritualistcentre.com/

NOW IT'S YOUR TURN

Discover the EXACT 3-step blueprint you need to become a bestselling author in 3 months.

Self-Publishing School helped me, and now I want them to help you with this FREE WEBINAR!

Even if you're busy, bad at writing, or don't know where to start, you CAN write a bestseller and build your best life.

With tools and experience across a variety niches and professions, Self-Publishing School is the only resource you need to take your book to the finish line!

DON'T WAIT

Watch this FREE WEBINAR now, and

Say "YES" to becoming a bestseller:

https://xe172.isrefer.com/go/affegwebinar/bookbrosinc6970/

Printed in Poland
by Amazon Fulfillment
Poland Sp. z o.o., Wrocław

54891577R00054